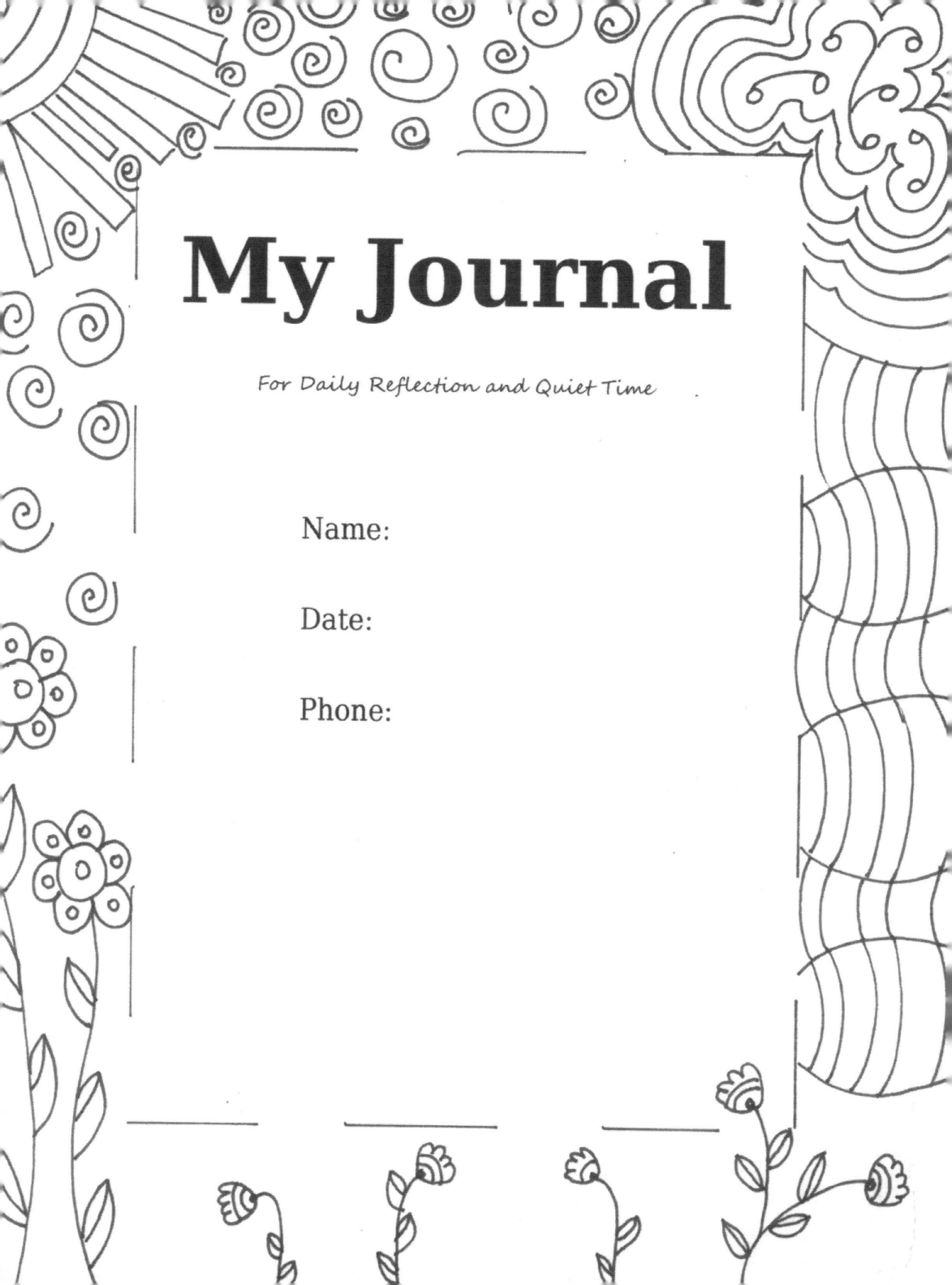

My Journal

For Daily Reflection and Quiet Time

by Leslie Monroe

Copyright Information

This work is for Home and Family use only. You may make copies of these materials for only the children in your household.

All other uses of this material must be permitted in writing by Monroe Liberty LLC. It is a violation of copyright law to distribute the electronic files or make copies for your friends, associates or students without our permission.

For information on using these materials for businesses, co-ops, school programs or churches please contact us for licensing.

Contact Us:

www.besimplybetter.com
attention Monroe Liberty LLC licensing

Instructions

This is your journal,

use it freely,

these are just suggestions.

The book is meant to be worked on weekly. There are planning pages that will help you plan your week. Then lots of space to write, draw, color and reflect. This is a gently guided journal, and is open to creative out pourings.

Write down quotes you want to remember and list books you are currently reading. This will be a lovely reflection of your life and what you are working through.

Focus on things that inspire you. Surround yourself with beauty, and let your mind and life be enriched by taking the time to be quiet.

Supplies:

Colored pencils, drawing pens,

milky gel pens, smooth tip markers

(Metallic pens and sharpie markers will bleed)

Get Ready for some FUN!

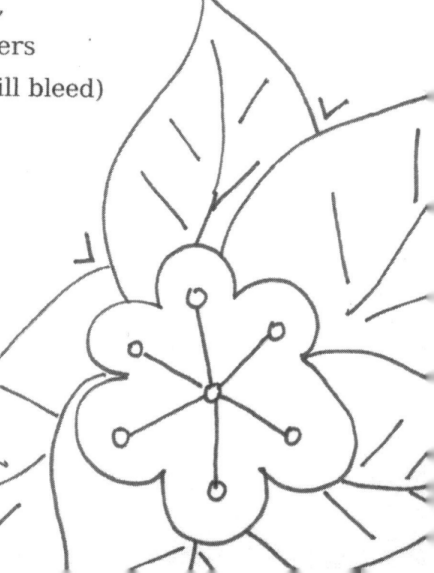

Month

Sunday	Monday	Tuesday	Wednesday

Year

Thursday	Friday	Saturday	Notes

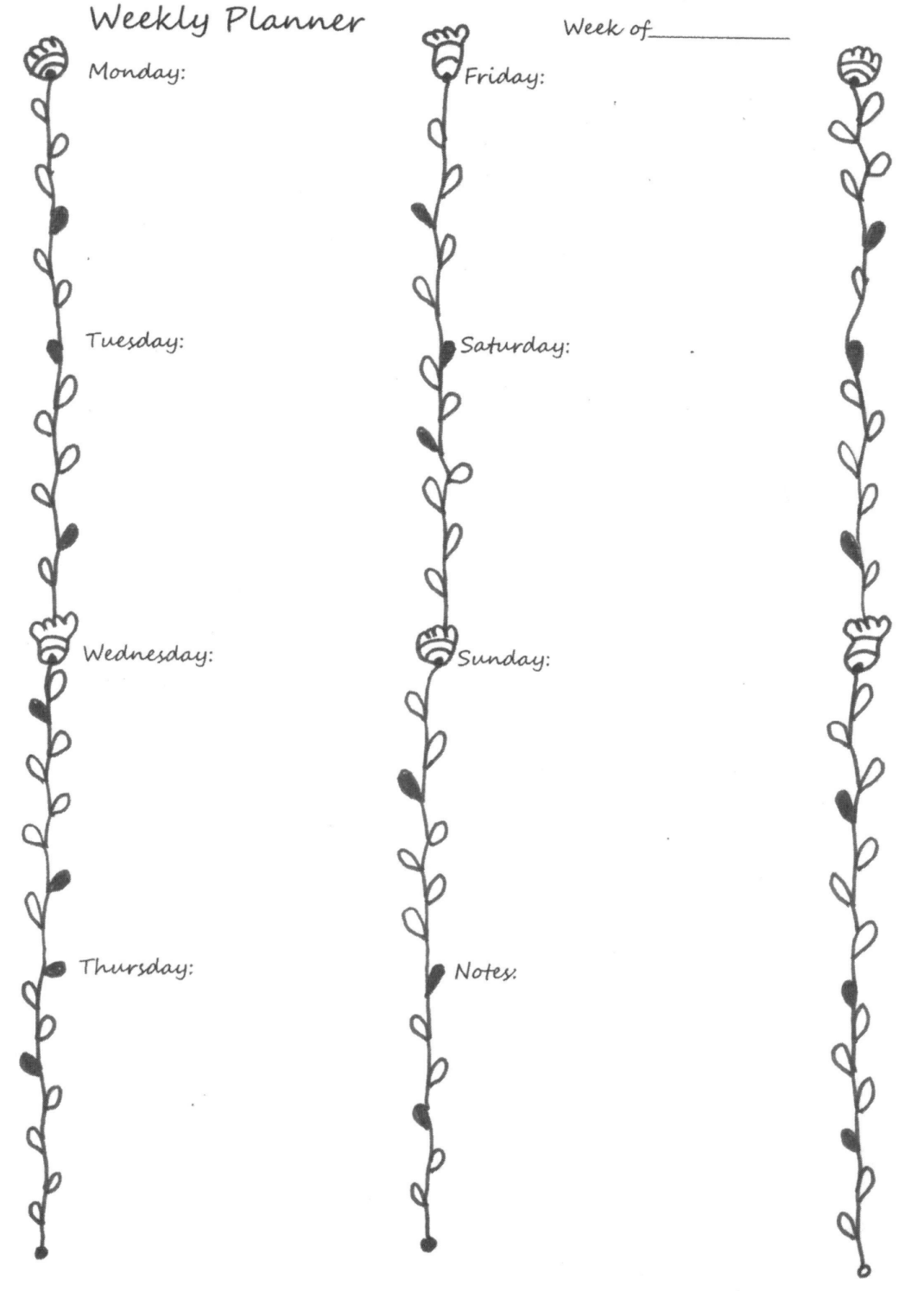

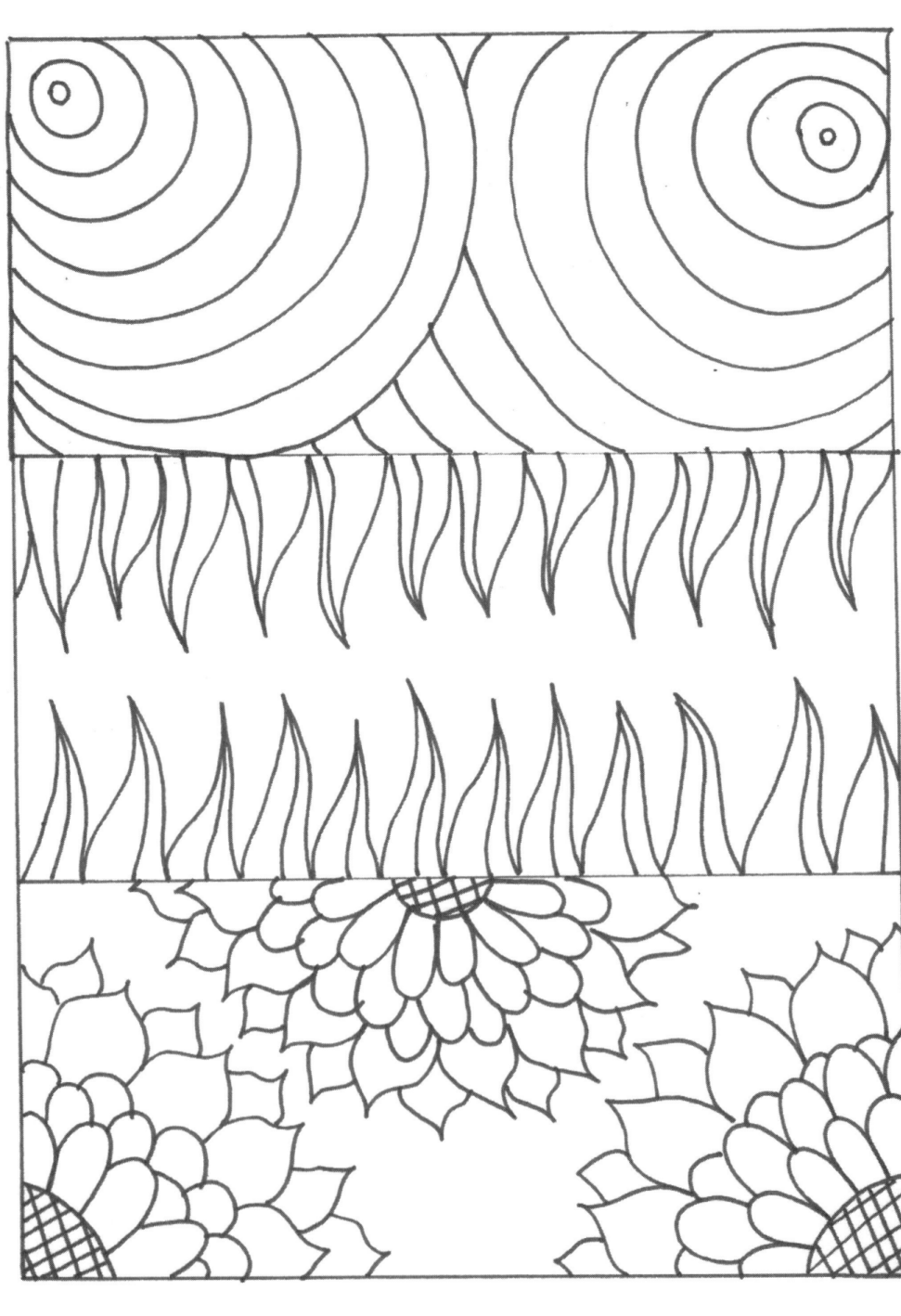

Weekly Planner

Week of_____

Monday:

Friday:

Tuesday:

Saturday:

Wednesday:

Sunday:

Thursday:

Notes:

Quotes to Remember, Ideas to reflect on

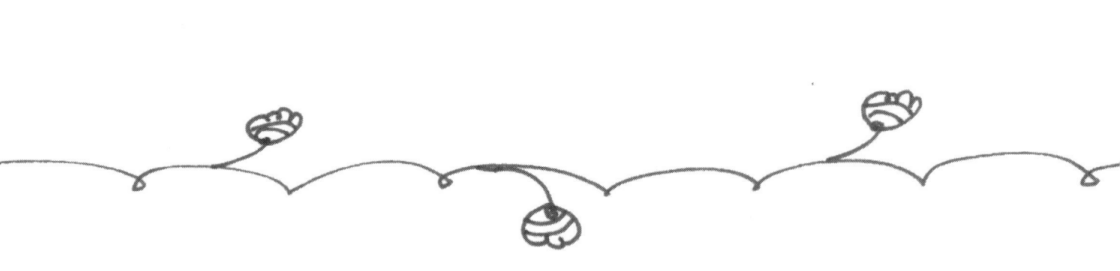

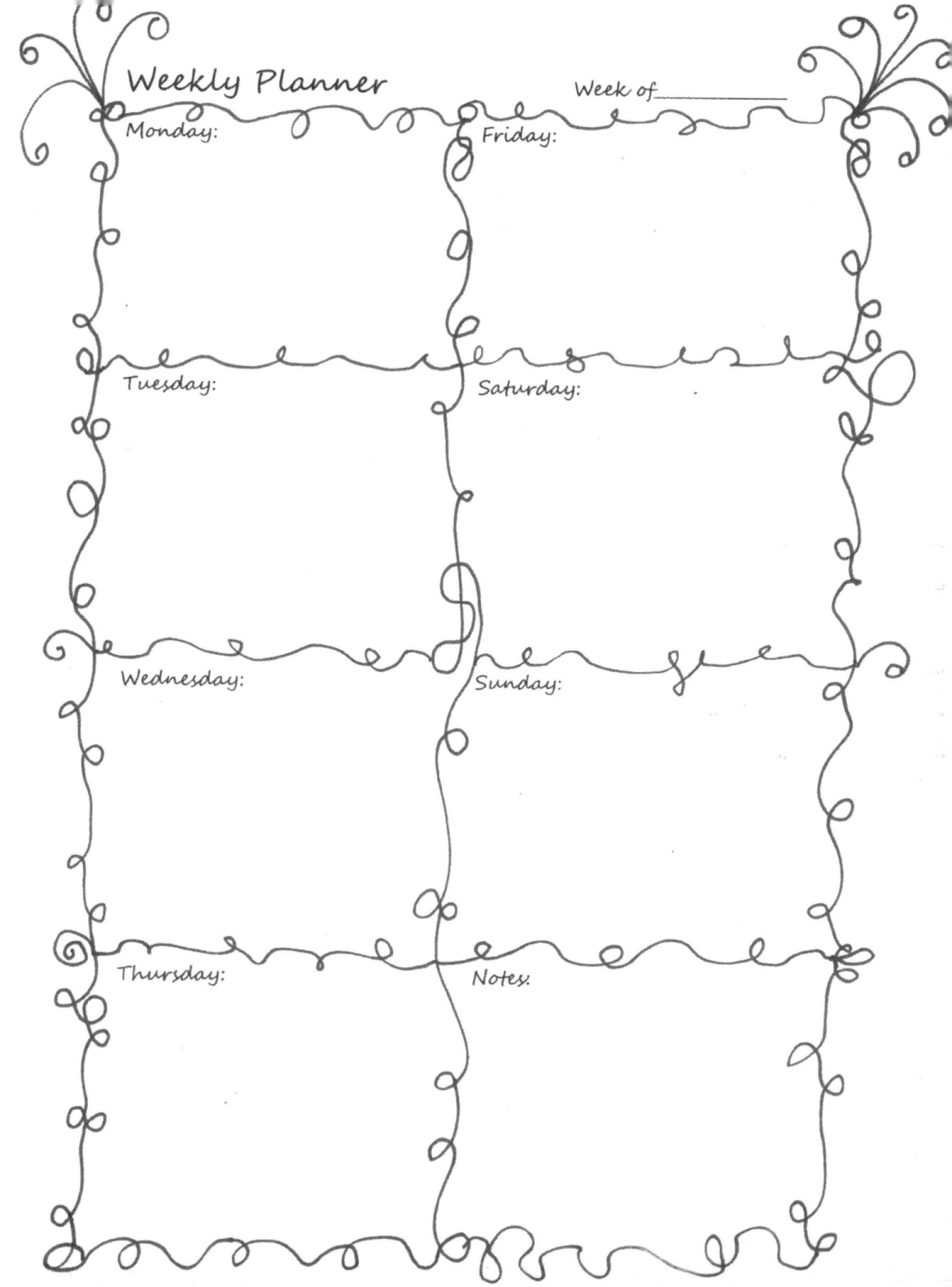

Thoughts to Remember

Weekly Planner

Week of_____

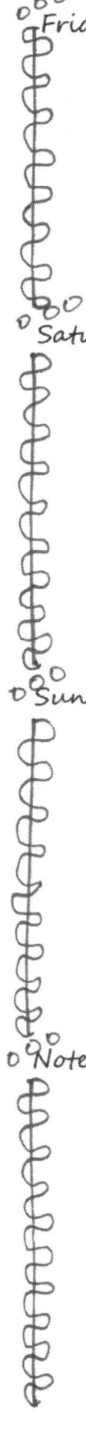

Monday:

Friday:

Tuesday:

Saturday:

Wednesday:

Sunday:

Thursday:

Notes:

Quotes to Remember, Ideas to reflect on

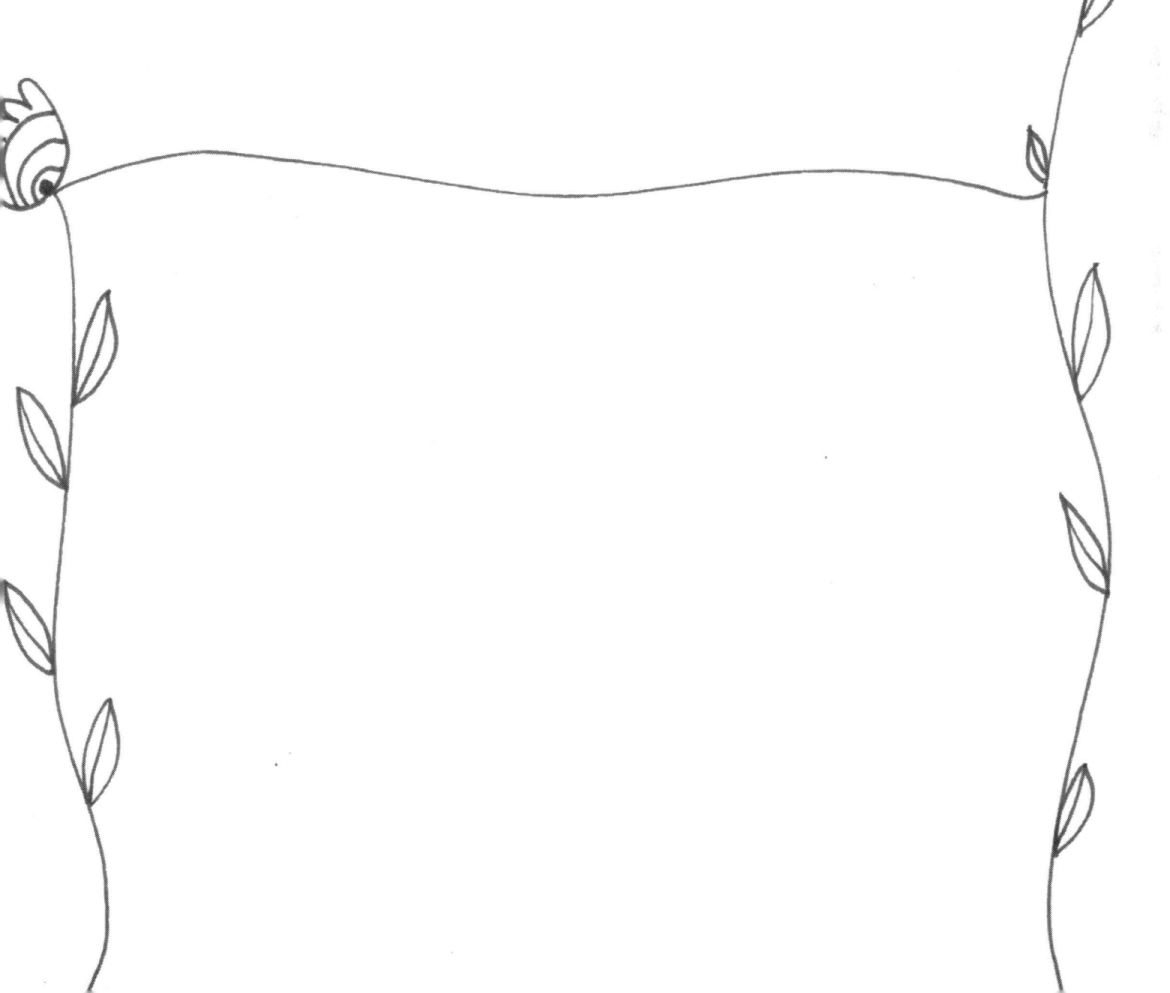

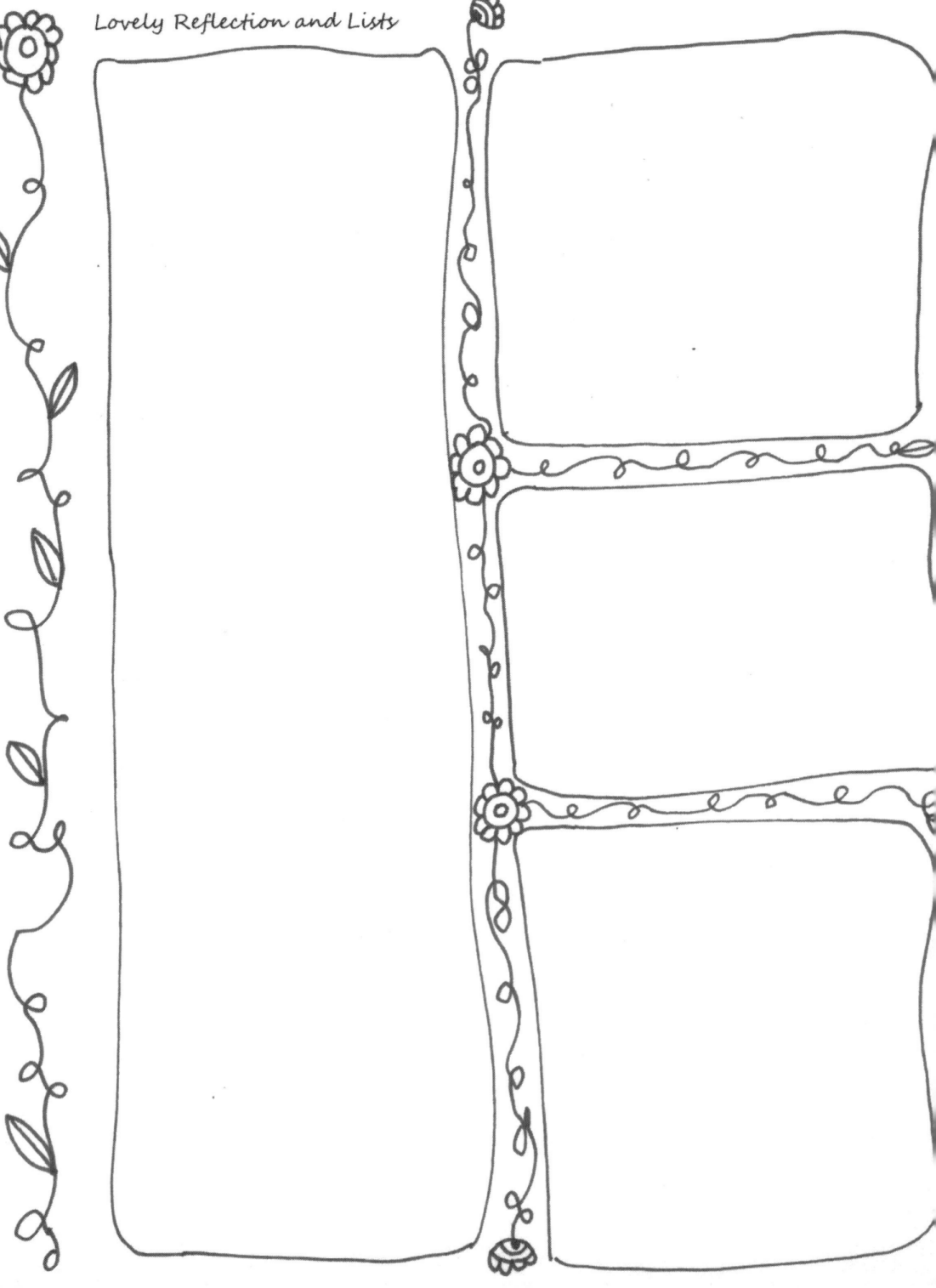

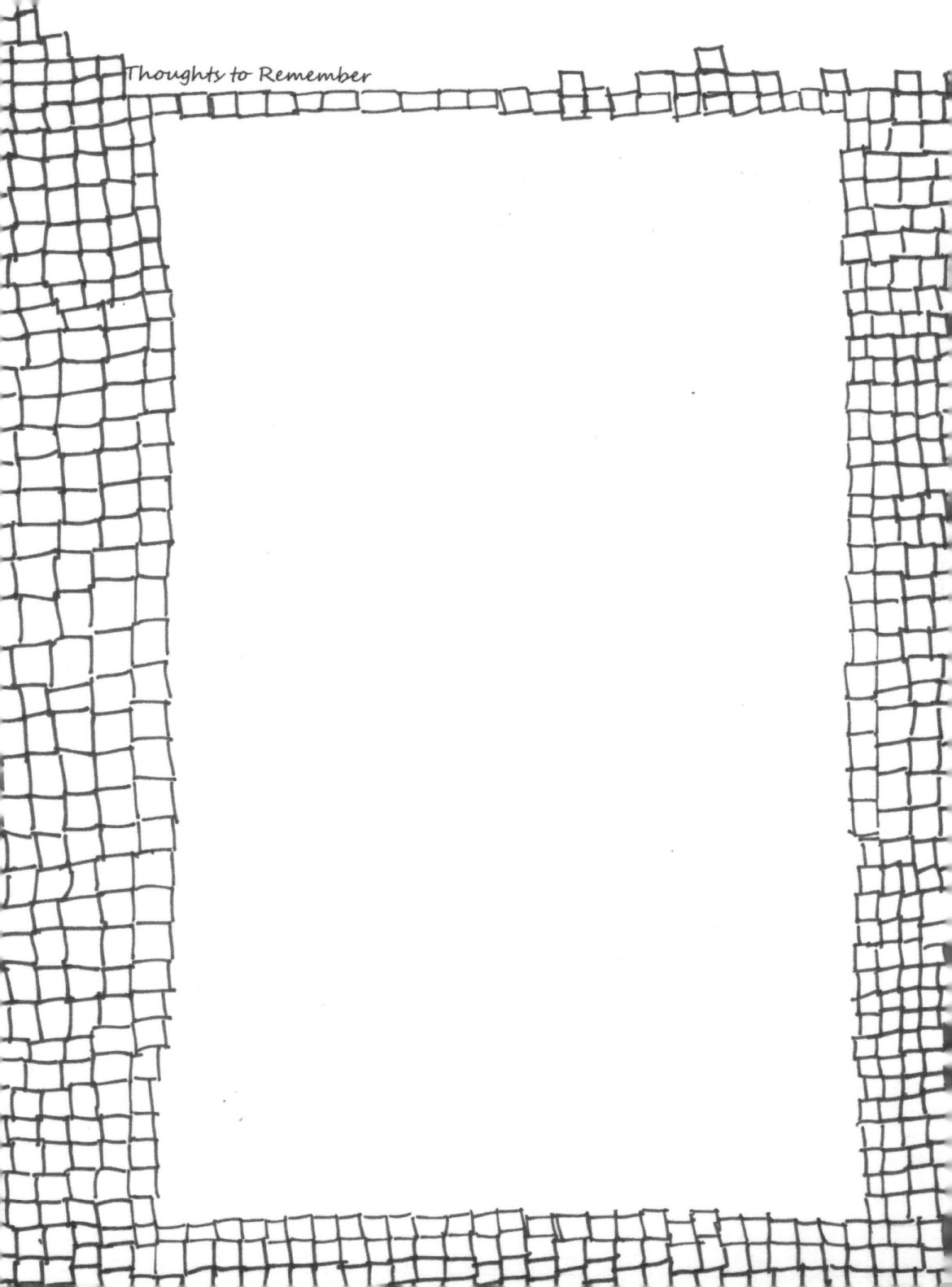

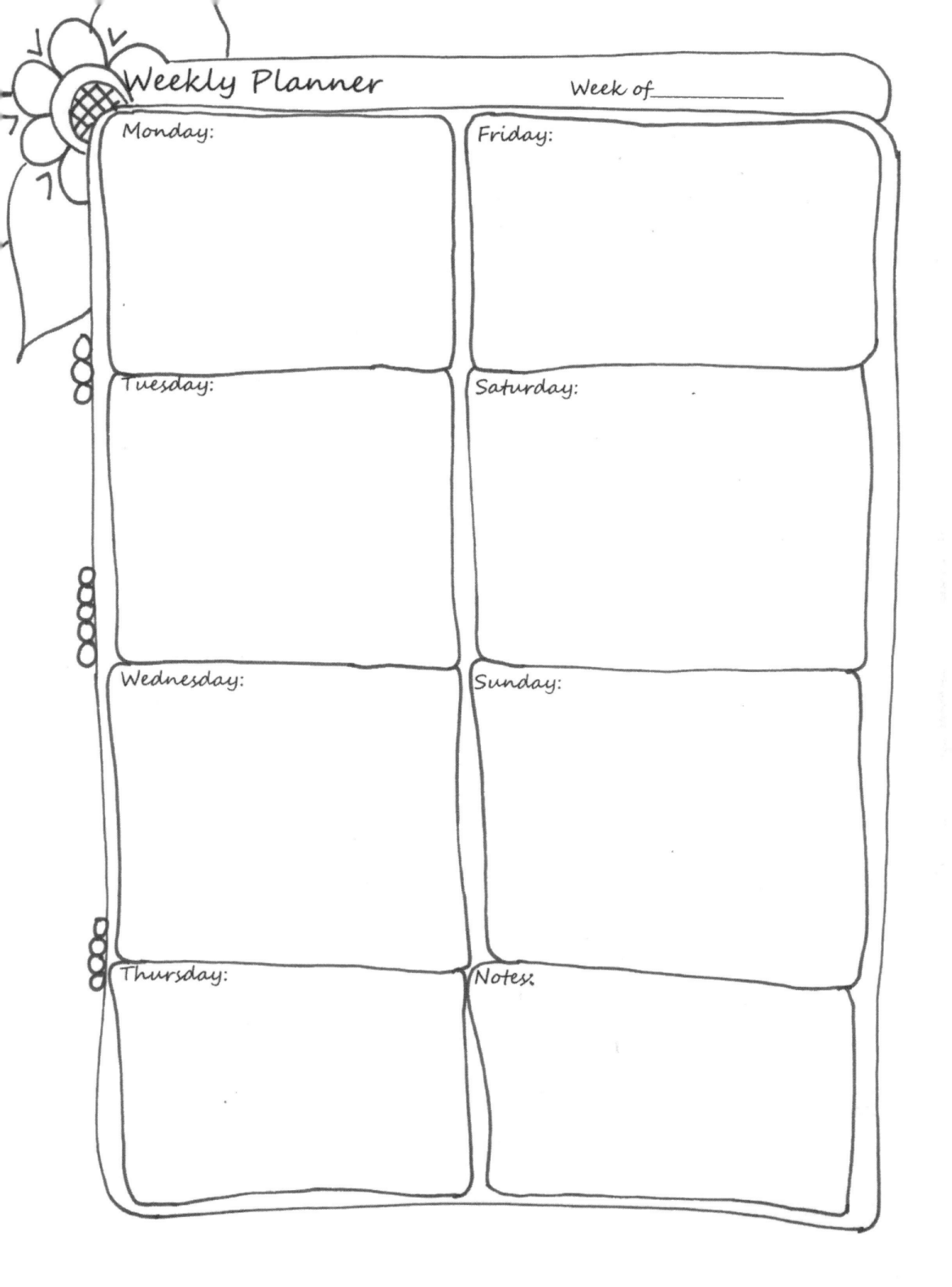

New Day for reflection and lists

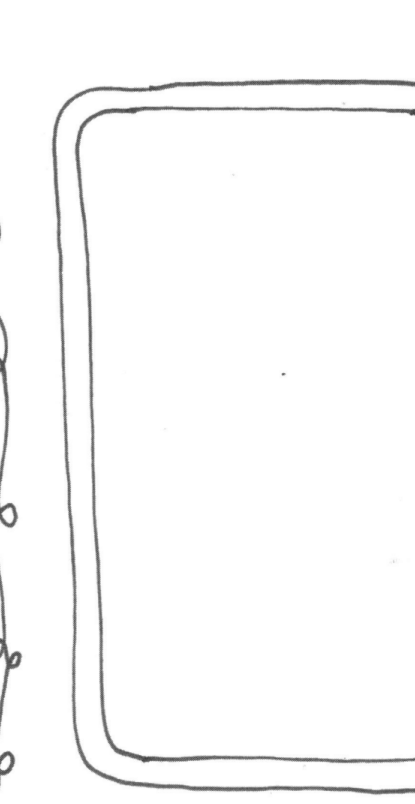

Audio coloring. Listen to an audio book, music or your favorite podcast. Color and draw as you let your mind absorb the content.

Reading List: I Want to Read all The Books!

Reading List: I Want to Read all The Books!

Reading List: I Want to Read all The Books!

○ _____

○ _____

○ _____

○ _____

○ _____

○ _____

○ _____

○ _____

○ _____

○ _____

○ _____

○ _____

○ _____

○ _____

○ _____

○ _____

○ _____

○ _____

○ _____

○ _____

○ _____

○ _____

○ _____

○ _____

○ _____

Important Dates to remember!

January

___

___

February

___

___

March

___

___

April

___

___

May

___

___

June

___

___

July

___

___

August

___

___

September

___

___

October

___

___

November

___

___

December

___

___